SCOTT JOPLIN
The King of Ragtime Writers
Easy Piano

Arranged by LAWRENCE GRANT

CONTENTS

COVER: Carol S. Wickham

© Copyright MCMLXXIV by Lewis Music Publishing Co., Inc.

International Copyright Secured   All Rights Reserved   Made in U. S. A.

THE ENTERTAINER

A RAG TIME TWO STEP

SCOTT JOPLIN
Arranged by Lawrence Grant

Not fast

© Copyright MCMLXXIV by Lewis Music Publishing Co., Inc.

International Copyright Secured   All Rights Reserved   Made in U.S.A.

The Entertainer 3-2

4

The Entertainer 3-3

To the Maple Leaf Club.

MAPLE LEAF RAG.

By King of Ragtime writers Scott Joplin.

Composer of
" Swipesy Cake Walk "
" Sunflower Slow Drag."

⑤

Published by

JOHN STARK & SON
ST. LOUIS, MO.
copyright 1899

MAPLE LEAF RAG

SCOTT JOPLIN
Arranged by Lawrence Grant

© Copyright MCMLXXIV by Lewis Music Publishing Co., Inc.

International Copyright Secured   All Rights Reserved   Made in U.S.A.

D. C. al Fine

Maple Leaf Rag -2

"THE EASY WINNERS"

A RAG TIME TWO STEP

SCOTT JOPLIN
Arranged by Lawrence Grant

Not fast

© Copyright MCMLXXIV by Lewis Music Publishing Co., Inc.

International Copyright Secured   All Rights Reserved   Made in U.S.A.

PEACHERINE RAG

SCOTT JOPLIN
Arranged by Lawrence Grant

Not too fast

© Copyright MCMLXXIV by Lewis Music Publishing Co., Inc.

International Copyright Secured   All Rights Reserved   Made in U.S.A.

Peacherine Rag-2

"BETHENA"

A CONCERT WALTZ

SCOTT JOPLIN
Arranged by Lawrence Grant

Valse cantabile

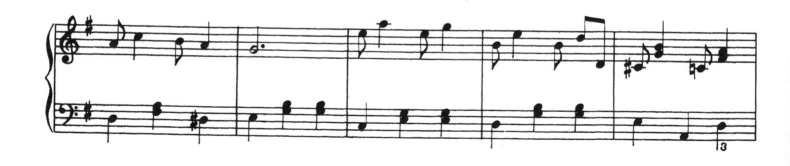

© Copyright MCMLXXIV by Lewis Music Publishing Co., Inc.

International Copyright Secured   All Rights Reserved   Made in U.S.A.

Bethena - 2

Bethena-3

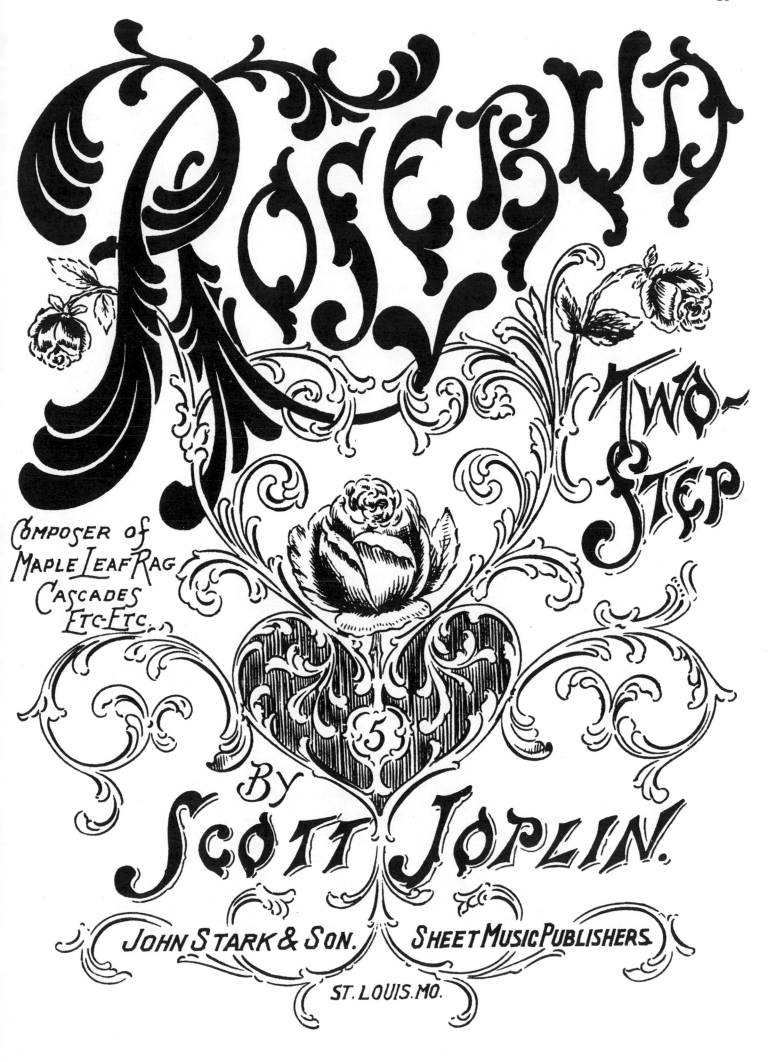

The Rose-bud March

SCOTT JOPLIN
Arranged by Lawrence Grant

Tempo di marcia

© Copyright MCMLXXIV by Lewis Music Publishing Co., Inc.

International Copyright Secured·   All Rights Reserved   Made in U.S.A.

Rose-bud March-2

Rose-Bud March -3

HARMONY CLUB

COPYRIGHT FOR All Countries.

WALTZ

BY

SCOTT JOPLIN.

Price 40 cents.

PUBLISHED BY ROBT SMITH, TEMPLE, TEX

LONDON, ENG., CHAS. SHEARD & Co.

HARMONY CLUB WALTZ

SCOTT JOPLIN
Arranged by Lawrence Grant

© Copyright MCMLXXIV by Lewis Music Publishing Co., Inc.

International Copyright Secured   All Rights Reserved   Made in U.S.A.

Harmony Club Waltz-2

SUN FLOWER SLOW DRAG

RAG TIME TWO STEP.

SCOTT JOPLIN & SCOTT HAYDEN
Arranged by Lawrence Grant

© Copyright MCMLXXIV by Lewis Music Publishing Co., Inc.

International Copyright Secured   All Rights Reserved   Made in U.S.A.

Sun Flower Slow Drag-2

THE STRENUOUS LIFE

A RAGTIME TWO STEP

SCOTT JOPLIN
Arranged by Lawrence Grant

© Copyright MCMLXXIV by Lewis Music Publishing Co., Inc.

International Copyright Secured'   All Rights Reserved   Made in U.S.A.

The Strenuous Life-2

ELITE SYNCOPATIONS

SCOTT JOPLIN
Arranged by Lawrence Grant

Not fast

to next page   *Fine*

© Copyright MCMLXXIV by Lewis Music Publishing Co., Inc.

International Copyright Secured   All Rights Reserved   Made in U.S.A.

D. C. al Fine

Elite Syncopations-2

THE CHRYSANTHEMUM

An Afro-American Intermezzo

SCOTT JOPLIN
Arranged by Lawrence Grant

Slow March Tempo

© Copyright MCMLXXIV by Lewis Music Publishing Co., Inc.

International Copyright Secured   All Rights Reserved   Made in U.S.A.

The Chrysanthemum-2

THE "RAG TIME DANCE"

SCOTT JOPLIN
Arranged by Lawrence Grant

Not fast

© Copyright MCMLXXIV by Lewis Music Publishing Co., Inc.

International Copyright Secured   All Rights Reserved   Made in U.S.A.

The Ragtime Dance-2

The Ragtime Dance-3